First Lessons Classical Guitar

by William Bay

Online Audio www.melbay.com/30048BCDEB

Audio Contents

Visit us on the Web at www.melbay.com — E-mail us at email@melbay.com

Preface

First Lessons® *Classical Guitar* is an innovative method. It will work well for the guitarist wanting to get started on his or her own and it also will work well in a studio/teaching situation. I begin in the key of A natural minor. The reason for this is that so much beautiful music is found in A minor. In addition, minor keys are especially rich on the classical guitar. Then we go into the relative major key to A minor, the key of C major. Next we venture into the key of E minor, another great key for classical guitar. Finally, we end with G major. A strength of this method is the abundance of melodies arranged for the beginning student. Upon completion of this method the student guitarist will have many interesting pieces to play in recital, concert or just for fun.

Table of Contents

How to Select a Guitar

When selecting a guitar it is important that you do not choose an instrument too big. Sometimes a 3/4 size nylon stringed guitar is the best instrument with which to begin your guitar study. Sit down, hold the instrument and make sure it feels comfortable to you. Check to make sure that there are not string buzzes in various places on up the fingerboard. This could indicate the presence of a high fret or perhaps a warp in the neck. Most student model guitars today are of a high quality, but it is best to have your teacher or another guitarist check out the instrument you hope to purchase.

The Guitar and its Parts

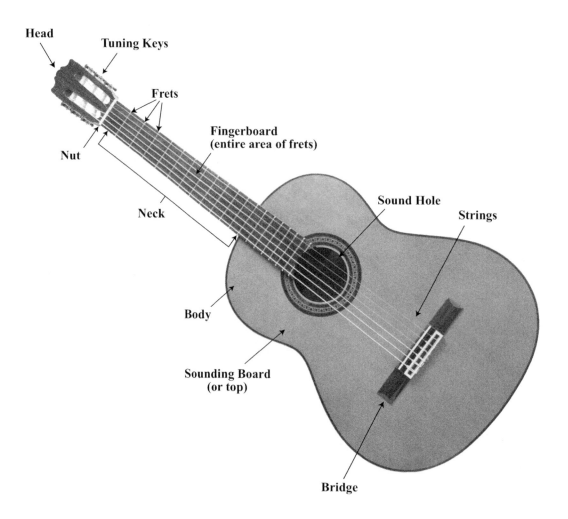

How to Hold the Guitar

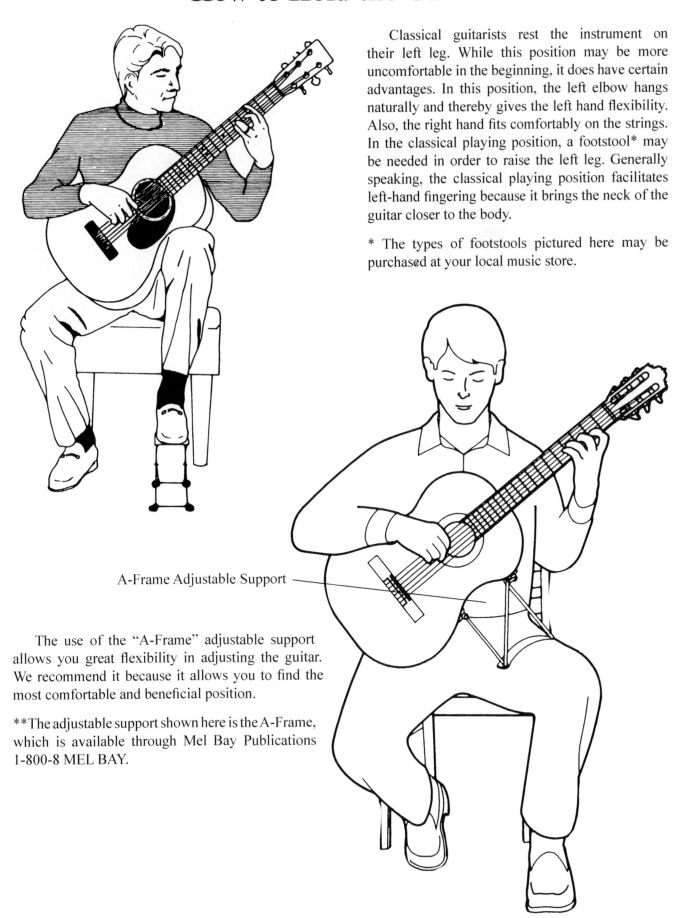

Classical guitarists rest the instrument on their left leg. While this position may be more uncomfortable in the beginning, it does have certain advantages. In this position, the left elbow hangs naturally and thereby gives the left hand flexibility. Also, the right hand fits comfortably on the strings. In the classical playing position, a footstool* may be needed in order to raise the left leg. Generally speaking, the classical playing position facilitates left-hand fingering because it brings the neck of the guitar closer to the body.

* The types of footstools pictured here may be purchased at your local music store.

A-Frame Adjustable Support —

The use of the "A-Frame" adjustable support allows you great flexibility in adjusting the guitar. We recommend it because it allows you to find the most comfortable and beneficial position.

**The adjustable support shown here is the A-Frame, which is available through Mel Bay Publications 1-800-8 MEL BAY.

Right Hand Position

The right arm should pivot approximately at the widest point on the instrument. Make certain that the elbow and wrist are loose. The right arm should feel comfortable to you. The tone will vary depending upon where the strings are plucked. The closer that you play on the fingerboard, the more mellow the tone. The sound is correspondingly sharper as we play closer to the bridge. The fingers should be held loosely so that flexibility can be attained. Make certain that your wrist and fingers are not held in a rigid, stiff manner.

Right Hand Fingers Touching String

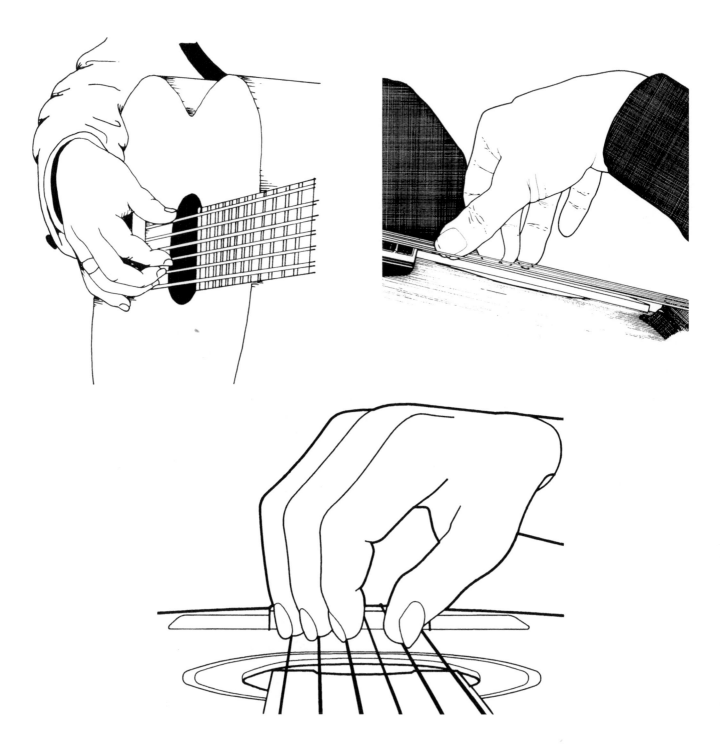

Left Hand Positioning

To begin with, keep the left elbow and wrist relaxed. Avoid positioning that strains and tightens your left wrist and elbow. The important thing to remember is to place the left hand so that the hand is arched and so that the fingers can fall straight down on the strings. Greater technique can be obtained by pressing down on the strings with the tips of the fingers than with the fleshy part. Also, it is important to bring the fingers directly down on the strings so that part of the finger does not accidentally touch and muffle one of the other strings.

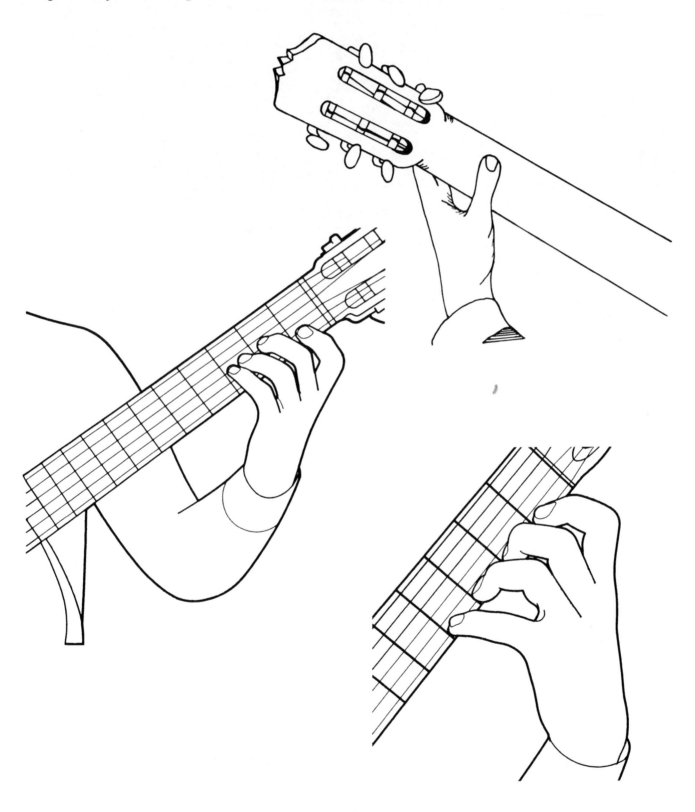

Tuning the Guitar

6th 1st
5th 2nd
4th 3rd

 Listen to track #1 of your audio and tune up as follows!

1st String – E

2nd String – B

3rd String – G

4th String – D

5th String – A

6th String – Low E

Electronic Guitar Tuner

Electronic Guitar Tuners are available at your local music store. They are a handy device and highly recommended.

Left Hand Fingering   Right Hand Fingering

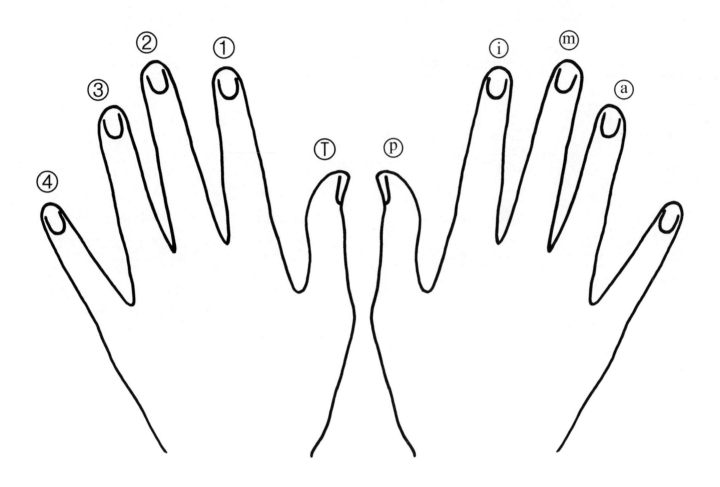

Right-hand finger symbols are derived from Spanish. The letters stand for:

Symbol	Spanish	English
p	Pulgar	Thumb
i	Índice	Index Finger
m	Medio	Middle Finger
a	Anular	Ring Finger

Note Values

When a note appears we play		When a rest appears, we do **not** play!	

Quarter note

Gets 1 beat

Draw quarter notes

A quarter note gets ___ beats?

Quarter rest

Gets 1 beat

Draw quarter rests

A quarter rest gets ___ beats?

Whole note

Gets 4 counts

Draw whole notes

A whole note gets ___ beats?

Whole note rest

Gets 4 beats

Draw whole note rests

A whole rest gets ___ beats?

notice that it hangs down from line 2

Half note

Gets 2 counts

Draw half notes

A half note gets ___ beats?

Half note rest

Gets 2 counts

Draw half note rests

A half note rest gets ___ beats?

notice that it sits upon line 3

Eighth note

Gets 1/2 beat

Draw eighth notes

An eighth note gets ___ beats?

Eighth rest

Gets 1/2 beat

Draw eighth rests

An eighth rest gets ___ beats?

Quiz

What kind of note? <u>Quarter</u> ____ ____ ____ ____ ____ ____ ____ ____ ____ ____

How many beats? <u>1</u> ____ ____ ____ ____ ____ ____ ____ ____ ____ ____

Counting

We will use the following **Time Signatures**.

4/4 or **C** Count: ‖ 1 —2 —3 —4 ‖   or   ‖ 1 and 2 and 3 and 4 and ‖

3/4 Count: ‖ 1 —2 —3 ‖   or   ‖ 1 and 2 and 3 and ‖

Notes
A – 5th String

A

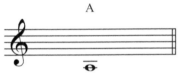

5th String Open

B

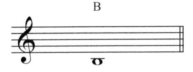

5th String, 2nd Fret

C

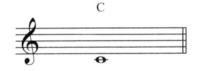

5th String, 3rd Fret

Track 2

5th String Study #1

Left Hand Fingers

5th String Study #2

Track 3

11

D – 4th String

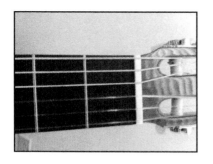  

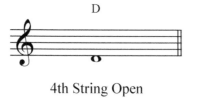

D

4th String Open

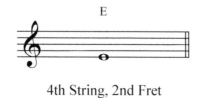

E

4th String, 2nd Fret

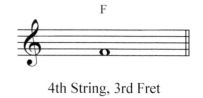

F

4th String, 3rd Fret

Track 4

4th String Study

4th String

Left Hand Fingers

Track 5

Notes on Two Strings

Track 6

Notes in 3/4 Time

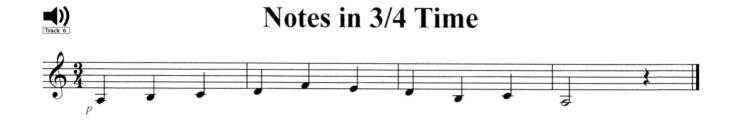

G – 3rd String

G

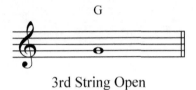

3rd String Open

A

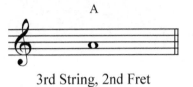

3rd String, 2nd Fret

Track 7

3rd String Study

Left Hand
Fingers

Track 8

A Natural Minor Scale

B – 2nd String

B

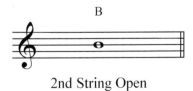

2nd String Open

C

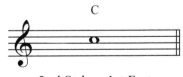
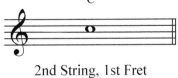

2nd String, 1st Fret

D

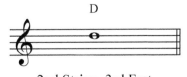

2nd String, 3rd Fret

13

2nd String Study #1

Left Hand
Fingers

2nd String Study #2

G String / B String

D String / G String / B String

Study on 4 Strings

E – 1st String

E

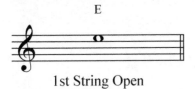

1st String Open

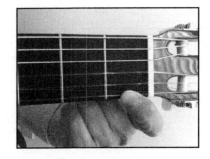

F

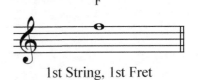

1st String, 1st Fret

G

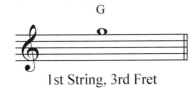

1st String, 3rd Fret

A

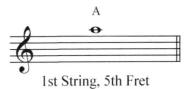

1st String, 5th Fret

E String Study #1

Track 14

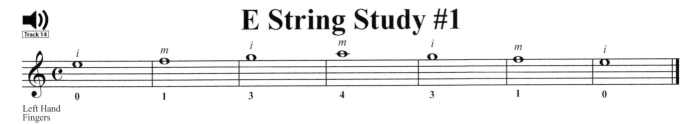

Left Hand Fingers

Dotted Half Note

A dotted half note receives 3 beats.

E String Study #2

Track 15

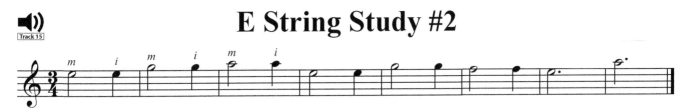

Track 16

A Natural Minor Scale in 2 Octaves

Low E – 6th String

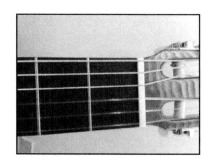

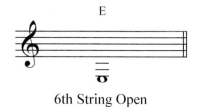

E

6th String Open

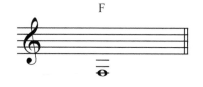

F

6th String, 1st Fret

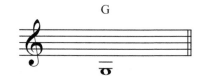

G

6th String, 3rd Fret

 Track 17

6th String Study

Left Hand
Fingers

 Track 18

Low Note Etude

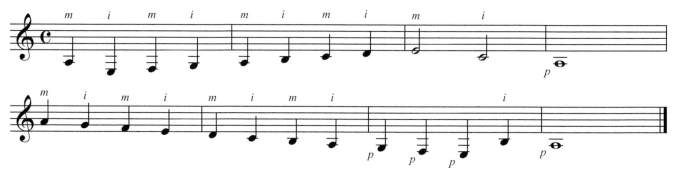

Autumn Waltz

Sunrise Meadow

Repeat Signs

Means to go back and repeat the phrase.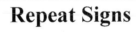

Repeat Waltz

G♯

Low G♯

6th String, 4th Fret

G♯

3rd String, 1st Fret

High G♯

1st String, 4th Fret

A Harmonic Minor Scale

Track 22

Left Hand Fingers

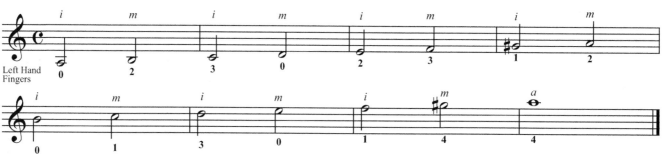

A Minor Arpeggios #1

Track 23

A Minor Arpeggios #2

Track 24

The Eighth Note

An **eighth note** receives one-half beat. (One quarter note equals two eighth notes.)

An eighth note will have a head, stem, and flag. If two or more are in successive order, they may be connected by a beam. (See example)

Pick-Up Notes

Some songs start with less than a full 4 beat measure. These starting notes are called a "Pick-up."

The time value of the pick-up note or notes is taken from the last measure of the piece.

Track 26

Morning Song

Accompaniment Chords

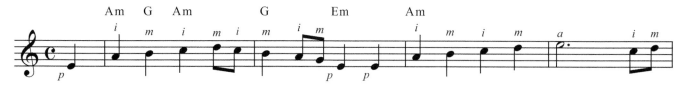

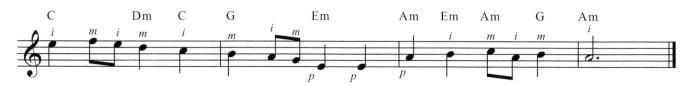

Track 27

Shady Grove

Accompaniment Chords

Track 28

Renaissance Dance

Accompaniment Chords

Chanson

Sakura

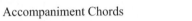

Playing Two Notes Together

French Carol

21

First and Second Endings

Sometimes two endings are used in certain selections…one to lead back into a repeated chorus and one to close it. They will be shown like this:

The first time, play the bracketed ending number 1. Repeat the chorus, and this time, skip the first ending and play ending number 2.

Track 32

Picardy

Dotted Quarter Note

A **dot** after a note increases its value by one-half.

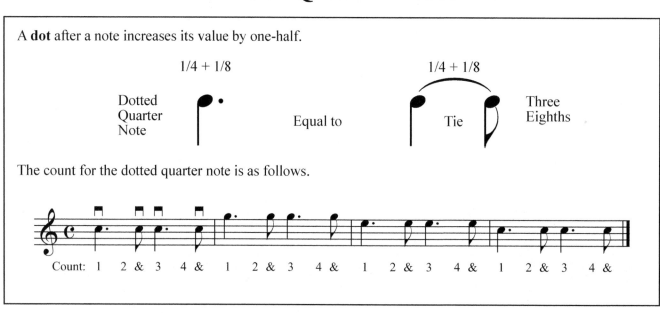

The count for the dotted quarter note is as follows.

22

Arcadian Melody

Star of the County Down

Playing Chords

Chord Study #1

Chord Study #2

Parson's Farewell

A Minor Arpeggios

①

②

③

④

⑤

Torino

Minuet

Key of C

C Major Scale

Track 41

Extended C Major Scale

Track 42

C Walks

Track 43

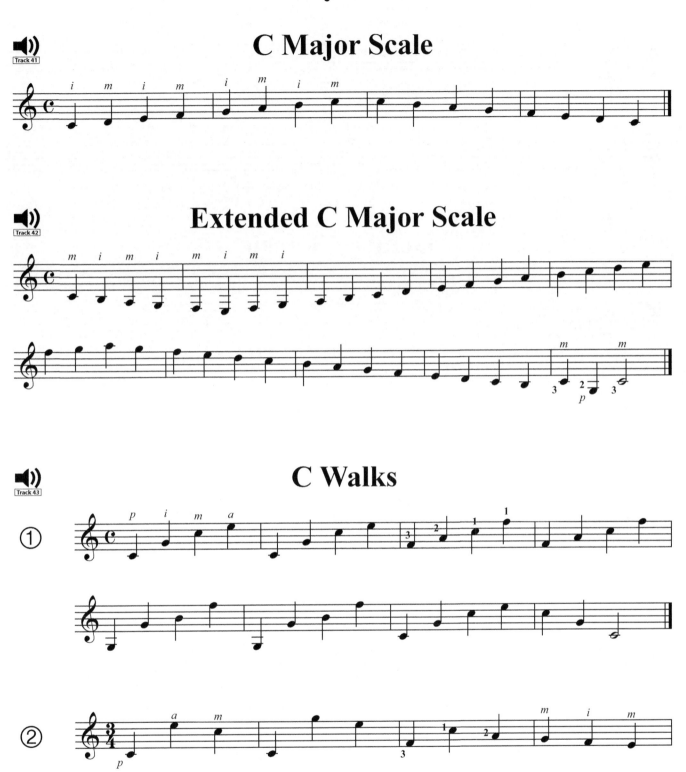

C Waltz

Track 44

Octave Chorale

Track 45

Early American Hymn

Track 46

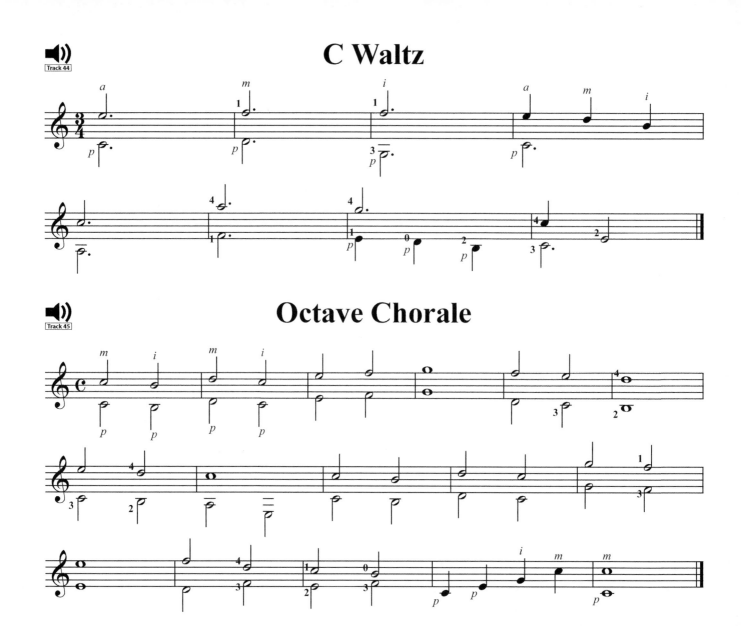

A tie is a curved line that joins two or more notes of the same pitch. When you see a tie, only pick the first note.

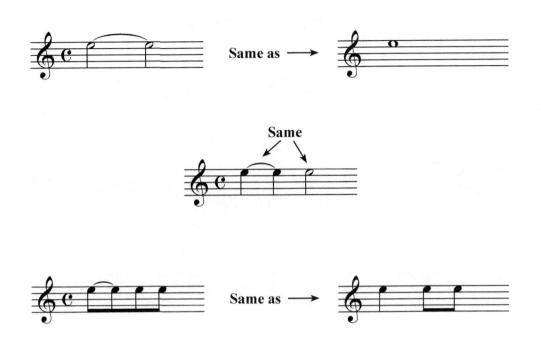

The Water is Wide

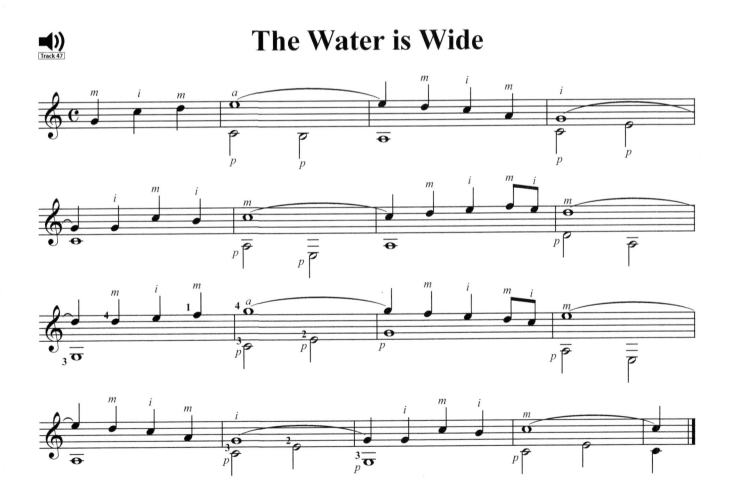

29

C Chords
Chord Study

Waltz in Two Parts

Triplets

A **triplet** is a group of three notes played in the time of two notes of the same kind.

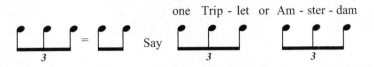

C Arpeggios

#1

#2

#3

F♯

Low F♯

F♯

High F♯

6th String, 2nd Fret

4th String, 4th Fret

1st String, 2nd Fret

Track 51

F♯ Etude

Left Hand Fingers

Track 52

What Child is This

32

Romance

Track 53

Hymn

Track 54

The Marsh of Rhuddlan

Track 55

Key Signature

When a sharp appears here all notes of that pitch will be sharped throughout the song unless a natural sign (♮) cancels the sharp.

E Minor

E Natural Minor Scale

Left Hand Fingers

E Minor Study

O Come, O Come Emmanuel

34

The Cuckoo

Johnny Has Gone for a Soldier

Shaker Dance

D♯

4th String, 1st Fret

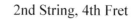

2nd String, 4th Fret

E Harmonic Minor Scale

Track 62

Left Hand Fingers

E Minor Walk

Track 63

E Minor Waltz

Track 64

Down in Yon Forest

Lament

37

E Minor Chords
Chord Study #1

Chord Study #2

Chord Study #3

E Minor Arpeggios

Nocturne

Andante

Key of G Major

Track 73

G Major Scale

Track 74

G Etude

Track 75

Thumb Study

41

Irish Hymn

Gilotte

Lagrima Theme

G Waltz

Prelude

Chords in G

Track 81
Chord Study #1

Track 82
Chord Study #2

Track 83
Chord Study #3

Track 84
Chord Study #4

G Arpeggio Studies

#1

#2

#3

#4

The South Wind

Musical Terms

Tempo Terms

Largo	Very Slowly
Lento	Slowly
Adagio	Slowly with a very expressive feeling
Andante	A walking speed, however not too fast
Moderato	Moderately, medium speed
Allegretto	Slightly more movement than Moderato
Allegro	Quickly, lively tempo, but not overly fast or "out of control"
Vivaci	Very fast
Rit. "Ritardando"	Slow down at a gradual rate
Acc. "Accelerando"	Accelerate or speed up at a gradual rate

Dynamics

pp	(pianissimo)	Very soft
p	(piano)	Soft
mp	(mezzo piano)	Medium soft
mf	(mezzo forte)	Medium loud
f	(forte)	Loud
ff	(fortissimo)	Very loud
◁	(crescendo)	Gradually get louder
▷	(decrescendo)	Gradually get softer
>	(accent)	The note is to be played louder

Phrasing Terms

8va	Play the notes one octave higher.
Staccato	Play the note(s) marked in a short detached manner.
Legato	Play the notes marked as a tick, or pluck the notes marked in a gentle, somewhat connected manner. Almost as if the notes are slurred.
Rubato	Very expressive, no set tempo, notes may be played longer or shorter than their exact value in order to add expression.
ad lib	Playing at liberty, playing in a totally free fashion, improvising or making up a melody if a given section is marked so in a piece.

For Further Study

Complete Method for Classic Guitar (Book)
by Mel Bay (Product ID: 93400)

Mel Bay's own method for the classic guitar, featuring a thorough grounding in the fundamentals of music and reading guitar notation, plus graded studies and pieces. This book presents classic guitar technique in a manner that anyone can easily follow. Musical and technical concepts are introduced gradually as needed throughout the text and driven home with ample musical illustrations. Information is provided on: basic right and left-hand techniques, reading standard notation, harmonics, and playing in various keys and positions. In addition to the many classical etudes included here by Aguado, Bach, Carcassi, Carulli, Diabelli, Giuliani, Sor, and others, Mel Bay has made a significant contribution to the student guitar repertoire by transcribing works by Bach, Brahms, Chopin, Mozart, Pleyel, Rubenstein, and others in the classical style. The pieces and exercises are arranged to progress systematically through various keys and playing positions. Written entirely in standard notation only.

Easy Classic Guitar Solos (Book)
by Mel Bay and Castle Joseph (Product ID: 93212)

Designed for the beginner, these diverse solos acquaint the student with musical selections by a myriad of great composers. Standard notation only.

Graded Repertoire for Guitar, Book One (Book/Audio Set)
by Stanley Yates (Product ID: 99630M)

This new series of graded repertoire for guitar has been put together with the aim of providing students with the most attractive, stylistically comprehensive, and inspiring music available, while at the same time realistically meeting the pedagogical needs of teachers. Students and teachers will therefore find in these volumes some of the most representative and attractive music of the major repertoire areas of the instrument, both historical and contemporary, carefully selected, graded and edited for pedagogical use. While some of this music is very well known, much of it is not to be found in similar collections. This volume includes easy music by Aguado, Carcassi, Carolan, Carulli, Domeniconi, Giuliani, Hudson, Koshkin, Manjón, Martz, Morlaye, Nava, Rameau, Rak, Ribayez, Shand, Sor, Tesar, Winner, Yates, York, and Zenamon.

Printed in Great Britain
by Amazon

83658802R00032